CHILDREN'S AUTHORS

YUYI MORALES

Jill C. Wheeler

ABDO Publishing Company

visit us at
www.abdopublishing.com

Published by ABDO Publishing Company, PO Box 398166, Minneapolis, Minnesota 55439.
Copyright © 2013 by Abdo Consulting Group, Inc. International copyrights reserved in all
countries. No part of this book may be reproduced in any form without written permission from the
publisher. The Checkerboard Library™ is a trademark and logo of ABDO Publishing Company.

Printed in the United States of America, North Mankato, Minnesota.
102012
012013

 PRINTED ON RECYCLED PAPER

Interior Photos: AP Images p. 20

Many thanks to Yuyi Morales and her family for the images on
the cover and pp. 5, 6, 7, 9, 11, 13, 15, 17, 19, 21

Series Coordinator: Megan M. Gunderson
Editors: Megan M. Gunderson, BreAnn Rumsch
Art Direction: Neil Klinepier

Cataloging-in-Publication Data

Wheeler, Jill C., 1964-
 Yuyi Morales / Jill C. Wheeler.
  p. cm. -- (Children's authors)
Includes bibliographical references and index.
ISBN 978-1-61783-576-6
1. Morales, Yuyi, 1968- --Juvenile literature. 2. Authors--Biography--Juvenile literature. 3. Women
authors--Biography--Juvenile literature. 4. Children's stories--Authorship--Juvenile literature. I.
Title.
813/.6--dc23
[B]

2012946367

CONTENTS

THE MAGIC OF BOOKS

Yuyi (JOO-jee) Morales grew up in Mexico. She dreamed of having light skin and blue eyes. She felt her brown skin and brown eyes made her less smart and beautiful. She did not always take pride in being a part of her **culture**.

Today, Morales still has brown skin and brown eyes. But now she knows how wonderful it can be to honor her rich culture. And no one doubts her talent as an author and illustrator. The **Pura Belpré Award** has honored her work five times!

Morales grew up speaking Spanish and then later learned English. So today, many of her books feature both languages. Her work celebrates her Mexican heritage with bright colors, fanciful stories, and folktales.

Morales believes books are like magic crystal balls. In them, she sees her past, present, and future. She sees what she loves and what she doesn't. She also sees her strengths and weaknesses. She hopes her readers also see themselves in the books they read.

Celebration is a major theme in Morales's stories and illustrations.

Mexican Childhood

Yuyi Morales was born on November 7, 1968, in Xalapa, Mexico. Yuyi was the first of four children. She grew up with her sisters, Elizabeth and Magaly, and her brother, Mario Alejandro.

Yuyi with her grandmother

Yuyi's father, Eligio Morales Fuentes, worked for the Mexican government. His dream was to help improve the lives of Mexican farmers. Yuyi's mother, Eloina Garcia Landa, was an elementary school teacher and a **psychotherapist**.

Yuyi's mother encouraged her children to

*Yuyi grew up in a home filled
with creative activity.*

learn arts and crafts. Yuyi began drawing at a younger age than her brothers and sisters. Yet she claims both Magaly and Mario were better at drawing than she was. Today, Magaly works as a children's book illustrator as well as a teacher.

Eloina taught Yuyi to sew and knit at a very young age. Yuyi used these skills to make clothes for her dolls. Yuyi also learned an important lesson from her mother. If she did not know how to do something, it was within her power to learn. This knowledge would be important later in Yuyi's life.

PICTURES AND MORE PICTURES

Yuyi was very young when she discovered her love of drawing. Her mother still has drawings Yuyi made as a toddler. Many of those drawings feature Yuyi as a young woman. In them, she has long hair, platform shoes, and a dog beside her.

Yuyi drew on whatever scraps of paper she could find. She copied pictures from postcards or cartoon magazines. Sometimes she stared at herself in the mirror to draw her own face. She studied family portraits and sketched pictures of her loved ones. Later, she doodled on school notebooks.

Yuyi also loved to copy pictures from graphic novels her parents bought. The stories were for grown-ups, but they included pictures. Yuyi dreamed of someday telling stories like those. But she never thought about becoming an artist. She did not yet believe something she loved to do could become her career.

In the meantime, Yuyi created handmade books. She folded pieces of paper together. Then, she wrote stories and drew pictures on the pages.

Yuyi loved drawing so much that her homework sometimes included more pictures than words. One art teacher even thought Yuyi's artwork was too good to be her own. However, Yuyi's father knew better. He thought perhaps her skills would help her become a talented **architect**.

Yuyi at age 5

Swimming to America

Yuyi discovered another talent while still a young girl. In addition to their creative pursuits, Yuyi and her sisters became competitive swimmers. They swam year-round in all kinds of conditions. On some winter days, the water was very cold. Yuyi could not curl her fingers or comb her hair afterward!

Swimming influenced Yuyi's educational plans, too. She graduated from Colegio Preparatorio de Xalapa in 1985. Then, she entered the University of Xalapa. She studied physical education and **psychology**. After graduation, Yuyi worked as a swimming coach.

Then, Yuyi met Tim O'Meara. Tim was from California. He was tall, he spoke Spanish, and he loved music. In time, he won Yuyi's heart. Eventually, Tim and Yuyi married and had a son named Kelly.

In 1994, Tim learned that his grandfather was very ill. His grandfather wanted to meet Yuyi and Kelly before he died. So, the family quickly packed and left for the United States.

To get her **visa**, Yuyi had to stay in the country for six months. That meant she had to leave behind her family, her swimming students, and Mexico. In California, Yuyi knew few people besides Tim who spoke Spanish. So, she focused on learning a new language and adjusting to a new life.

Kelly, Yuyi, and Tim

Making Magic

Immigration rules did not allow Morales to get a job right away. So, she stayed home with Kelly. They spent time with her husband's mother. She spoke only English, but this didn't stop her from changing Morales's life. One day, she took Morales to the local public library.

In the children's section, Morales found herself surrounded by works of art blended with stories. The beautiful pictures meant she did not even need to read English to know what was happening.

Morales had enjoyed some children's books in Mexico. There had been Walt Disney stories, coloring books, and comic books. Yet they were nothing like what she found in the library in California.

Suddenly, Morales had a new passion. She decided to learn how to create her own works of art with stories. She also needed to learn to write in English so more people could share

Morales learned how to bind books, make paper, and do many other things from library books.

in her stories. Television shows such as *Sesame Street* and *Reading Rainbow* helped Morales learn English.

Most of Morales's earlier artwork was drawn in pen or pencil. She had done very little painting. So, she bought her first set of paints and brushes and began teaching herself. Her first paintings illustrated a story about her baby son. She bound the pages like a book and made the paper for the cover herself.

BECOMING AN ILLUSTRATOR

Morales was driven to learn everything she could about art and books. She carefully studied the books she saw in the library. She practiced painting by copying the work of artists she admired. Morales also signed up for conferences and evening classes on writing and illustrating.

Morales discovered that writing and painting made her feel a little less homesick. She filled pages with Mexican colors, clothes, foods, and celebrations. In this way, she could experience some of the things she missed about home.

Painting was not Morales's only artistic interest. In 1997, she created a weekly Spanish-language children's radio program in San Francisco, California. She spent three years hosting the show. It featured legends and myths from Latin

America. Then in 1998, Morales helped found a writer's group called the Revisionaries.

In 2000, Morales won a **grant** for her illustrations. Soon after, her first book was published. Her illustrations appeared in *Todas las Buenas Manos* by author F. Isabel Campoy.

Morales has a beautiful workspace in her home. She and her husband designed the studio, which opens out onto a garden.

A Not-So-Scary Skeleton

Morales's work was published again in 2003. She illustrated *Harvesting Hope: The Story of Cesar Chavez*. This biography of Mexican labor leader and activist Chavez is by Kathleen Krull. Critics praised the book and Morales's illustrations. *Child* magazine, *School Library Journal*, and *Booklist* named it one of the best books of the year.

That same year, Morales was thrilled to publish *Just a Minute: A Trickster Tale and Counting Book*. She both wrote and illustrated the book.

In the book, Grandma Beetle answers the door to find death waiting for her. Death is in the form of a skeleton named Señor Calavera. He wants to take Grandma Beetle to the afterlife, but she has other plans. It is her birthday, and she's busy getting ready for a party!

Each year, Mexicans celebrate the **Day of the Dead** with candy skulls and toy skeletons. Yet a children's book about death had made American publishers uneasy. But Morales's work won more than a dozen honors! These included a **Pura Belpré Award** Medal for its illustrations.

In 2008, Morales published another story about Señor Calavera. In *Just In Case: A Trickster Tale and Spanish Alphabet Book*, he searches for the perfect birthday gift for Grandma Beetle.

Señor Calavera means "Mr. Skull."

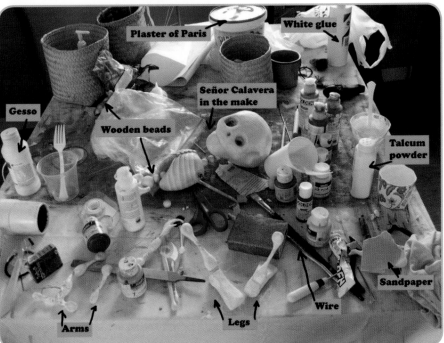

Plaster of Paris

White glue

Gesso

Señor Calavera in the make

Wooden beads

Talcum powder

Arms

Legs

Wire

Sandpaper

More Tales to Tell

Morales returned to illustrating books for other authors for her next projects. *Sand Sister* by Amanda White was published in 2004. It is the story of a lonely girl's day at the beach.

Then in 2006, *Los Gatos Black on Halloween* by Marisa Montes was published. Morales's illustrations help tell the story of a Halloween party at a haunted house. It features characters from Mexican history and folktales. It also includes Morales's aunts as witches and her family as skeletons! *Los Gatos Black* won a **Pura Belpré Award** Medal for Morales's images.

Morales's next book, *Little Night*, is the story of a hide-and-seek game between Mother Sky and Little Night. Morales wrote and illustrated the book because of her writing group. Members challenged themselves to write about a lost thing and hairdos. Morales's mother had loved to do her children's hair. But Elizabeth would run and hide when it was her turn!

In 2010, *My Abuelita* was finally published. It took Morales three years to illustrate this story by Tony Johnston. She built puppets for the characters. She sewed

Los Gatos Black *and* Little Night *are written in both English and Spanish. This helps Morales's work reach many readers.*

their clothes and made their furniture. Then, she and her husband propped up the puppets and photographed them.

Finally, Morales scanned the pictures into her computer and added facial expressions and other details. She also blended each photograph with backgrounds she had painted. *My Abuelita* was selected as a **Pura Belpré Award** Honor Book for these illustrations.

HARDWORKING ARTIST

Today, Morales and her husband and son live in the San Francisco Bay Area. Tim is a computer software engineer and a photographer. Kelly enjoys playing basketball. He is also passionate about music.

Morales spends most of her day drawing and painting. She also answers emails, gives interviews, and visits schools. And, she meets with her writing group twice a month. She also enjoys gardening and Brazilian dance classes.

Morales balances time as a wife and mother with time as a writer and illustrator. It takes 60 to 80 hours to paint a single illustration for a picture book. That means one book can take her more than seven months to paint!

Soetoro-Ng is President Barack Obama's sister.

For 2011, Morales illustrated a book by Maya Soetoro-Ng. Soetoro-Ng's story, *Ladder to the Moon*, is inspired by her daughter. It is about a little girl who gets to meet the grandmother she never knew in a dream. Morales's dreamlike illustrations are the perfect backdrop for this magical story.

Morales knows there are stories living inside her. She just has to sit, be patient, and write and write. Then the stories will start coming out. Readers look forward to seeing what flows out of her creative mind next!

Morales has done book signings and readings at conferences and schools.

GLOSSARY

architect - a person who plans and designs buildings. His or her work is called architecture.

culture - the customs, arts, and tools of a nation or a people at a certain time.

Day of the Dead - a Mexican holiday that honors the dead. It is usually celebrated on November 2.

grant - a gift of money to be used for a special purpose.

immigration - relating to entry into another country to live.

psychology (seye-KAH-luh-jee) - the science of the mind and behavior.

psychotherapist (seye-koh-THEHR-uh-pihst) - a person who treats mental or emotional illnesses by talking rather than using medicines.

Pura Belpré Award - an annual award given by the American Library Association. It honors Latino and Latina writers and illustrators whose work for children celebrates the Latino cultural experience. Winners receive the Pura Belpré Medal. Runners-up are called Pura Belpré Award Honor Books.

visa - a stamp on a passport that allows a person to enter and leave a certain country.

WEB SITES

To learn more about Yuyi Morales, visit ABDO Publishing Company online. Web sites about Yuyi Morales are featured on our Book Links page. These links are routinely monitored and updated to provide the most current information available.
www.abdopublishing.com

INDEX